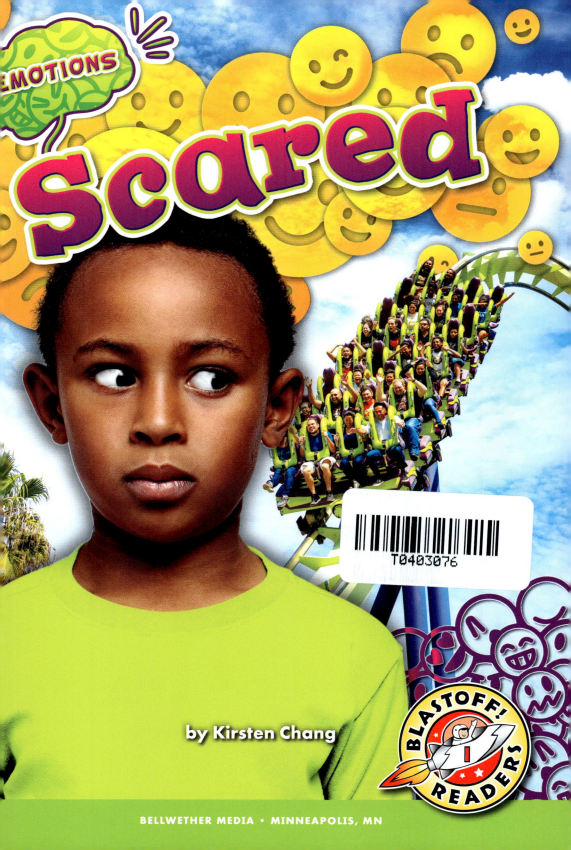

Blastoff! Readers are carefully developed by literacy experts to build reading stamina and move students toward fluency by combining standards-based content with developmentally appropriate text.

 Level 1 provides the most support through repetition of high-frequency words, light text, predictable sentence patterns, and strong visual support.

 Level 2 offers early readers a bit more challenge through varied sentences, increased text load, and text-supportive special features.

 Level 3 advances early-fluent readers toward fluency through increased text load, less reliance on photos, advancing concepts, longer sentences, and more complex special features.

★ **Blastoff! Universe**

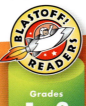

This edition first published in 2025 by Bellwether Media, Inc.

No part of this publication may be reproduced in whole or in part without written permission of the publisher. For information regarding permission, write to Bellwether Media, Inc., Attention: Permissions Department, 6012 Blue Circle Drive, Minnetonka, MN 55343.

Library of Congress Cataloging-in-Publication Data

LC record for Scared available at: https://lccn.loc.gov/2024014735

Text copyright © 2025 by Bellwether Media, Inc. BLASTOFF! READERS and associated logos are trademarks and/or registered trademarks of Bellwether Media, Inc. Bellwether Media is a division of Chrysalis Education Group.

Editor: Rebecca Sabelko   Designer: Andrea Schneider

Printed in the United States of America, North Mankato, MN.

Table of Contents

I Am Scared	4
What Is Fear?	6
Being Scared	14
Glossary	22
To Learn More	23
Index	24

I Am Scared

Riley is in bed.
It is dark.
She feels scared.

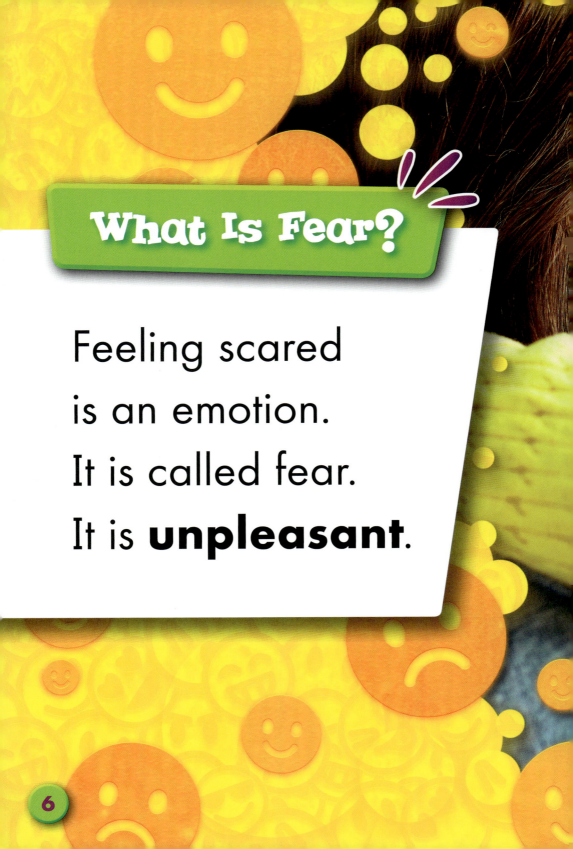

What Is Fear?

Feeling scared is an emotion. It is called fear. It is **unpleasant**.

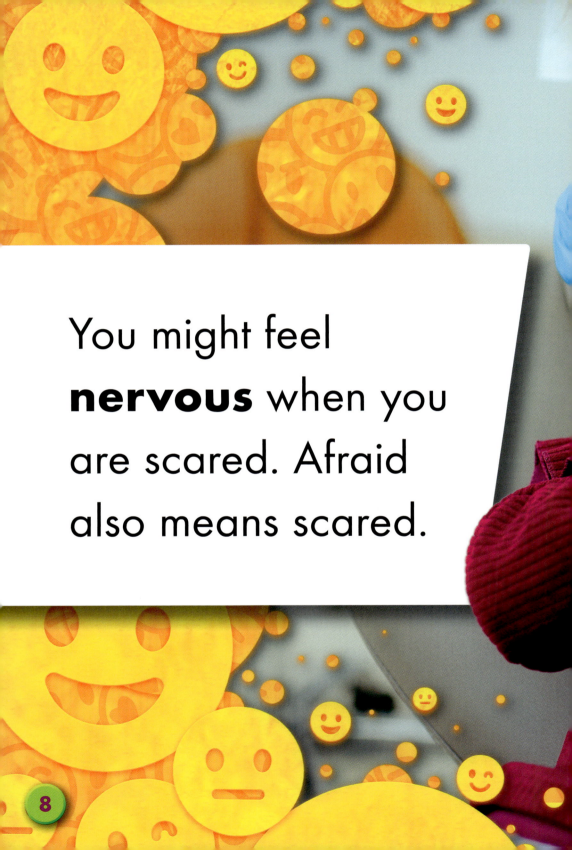

You might feel **nervous** when you are scared. Afraid also means scared.

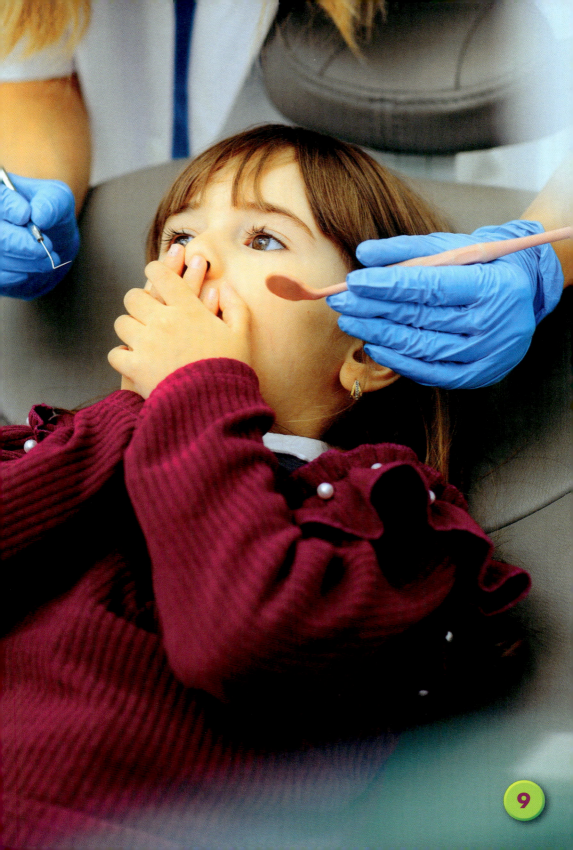

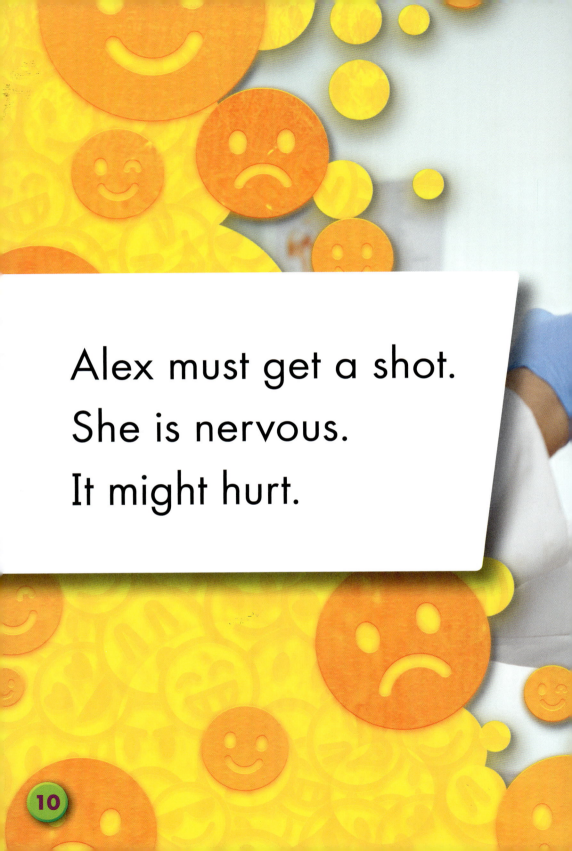

Alex must get a shot.
She is nervous.
It might hurt.

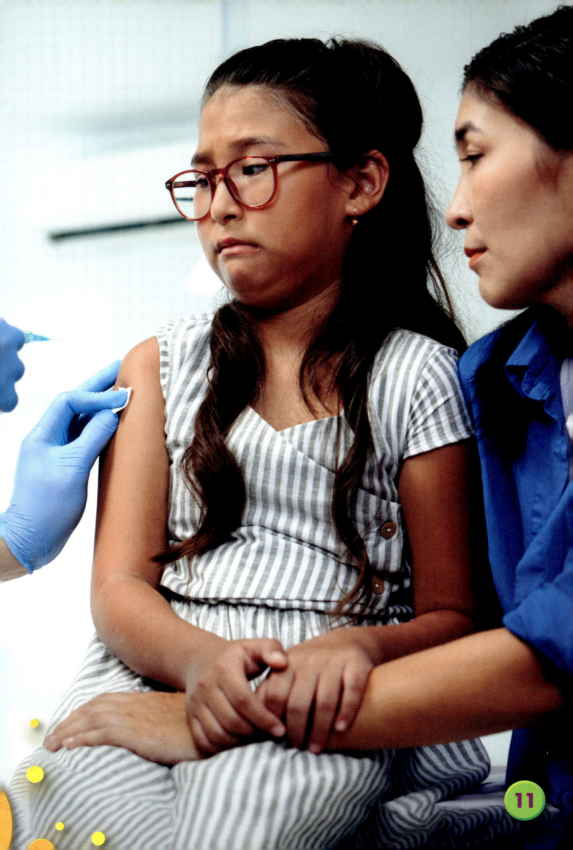

Irie climbed a tree.
Now she is afraid.
It feels **dangerous**.

Being Scared

Ollie is scared. He hides behind the couch.

Bella is afraid. She screams!

Being scared can make your heart beat faster.
You may **sweat**.
You may breathe fast.

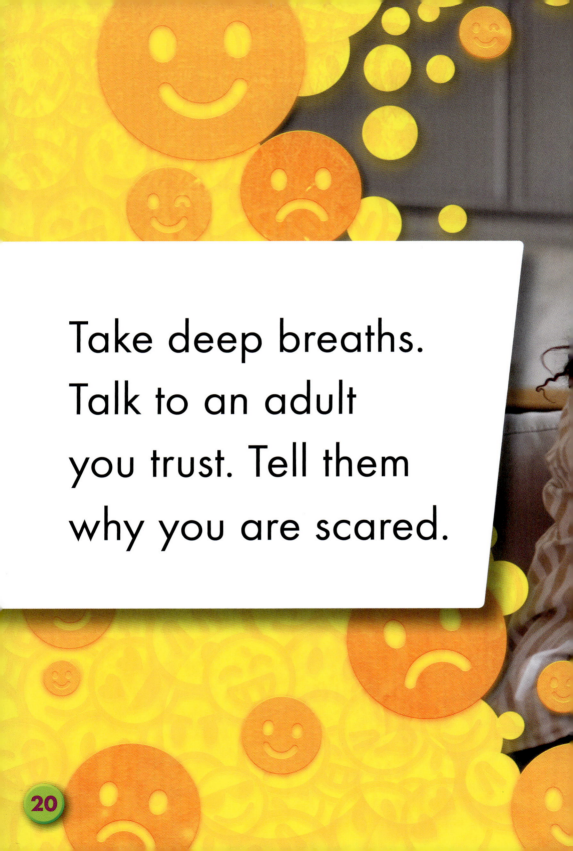

Take deep breaths. Talk to an adult you trust. Tell them why you are scared.

Glossary

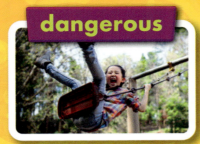

dangerous

not safe

sweat

to give off a salty liquid through the skin

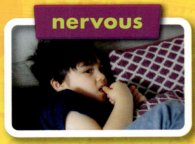

nervous

uncomfortable or fearful

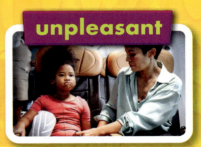

unpleasant

not nice

To Learn More

AT THE LIBRARY

Chang, Kirsten. *Understanding Emotions*.
Minneapolis, Minn.: Bellwether Media, 2022.

Culliford, Amy. *Scared*. New York, N.Y.:
Crabtree Publishing, 2021.

Mansfield, Nicole A. *Sometimes I Feel Scared*.
North Mankato, Minn.: Pebble, 2022.

ON THE WEB

FACTSURFER

Factsurfer.com gives you
a safe, fun way to find
more information.

1. Go to www.factsurfer.com.

2. Enter "scared" into the search box
   and click Q.

3. Select your book cover to see
   a list of related content.

Index

adult, 20
afraid, 8, 12, 16
bed, 4
breathe, 18, 20
couch, 14
dangerous, 12
dark, 4
emotion, 6
fear, 6
feels, 4, 6, 8, 12
heart, 18
hides, 14
hurt, 10
identify fear, 17
nervous, 8, 10
question, 21
screams, 16
shot, 10
sweat, 18, 19
talk, 20
tree, 12
unpleasant, 6
why are you scared, 13

The images in this book are reproduced through the courtesy of: Anatoliy Karlyuk, front cover (scared child); Cassiohabib, front cover (background); Suresh Heyt/peopleimages.com, p. 3; SB Arts Media, pp. 4-5; A.D.S.Portrait, pp. 6-7; Nicoleta Ionescu, pp. 8-9; DragonImages, pp. 10-11; phatpc, pp. 12-13; kryzhov, p. 13 (being in the dark); Fly View Productions, p. 13 (getting a shot); Marius Pirvu, p. 13 (doing dangerous things); Caven Images/ Alamy, pp. 14-15; Juriah Mosin, pp. 16-17; Artsplav, p. 17 (hiding); SolStock, p. 17 (screaming); globalmoments, p. 17 (sweating); Maximumm, pp. 18-19; Prostock-studio, pp. 20-21; Hakase_, p. 22 (dangerous); Ann in the uk, p. 22 (nervous); Kanthita, p. 22 (sweat); Stella, p. 22 (unpleasant); Lightfield Studios, p. 22 (scared child).